Help Me **Understand**

What Happens When My Parent Is in Jail?

Frank Felice

PowerKiDS press.

NEW YORK

Published in 2019 by The Rosen Publishing Group, Inc.
29 East 21st Street, New York, NY 10010

First Edition

Editor: Elizabeth Krajnik
Book Design: Rachel Rising

Photo Credits: Cover, sirtravelalot/Shutterstock.com; p. 4 ktmoffitt/E+/Getty Images; p. 5 Skyward Kick Productions/Shutterstock.com; p. 6 Africa Studio/Shutterstock.com; p. 7 wavebreakmedia/Shutterstock.com; p. 9 iko/Shutterstock.com; p. 10 yurchello108/Shutterstock.com; p. 11 Justin Sullivan/Getty Images News/Getty Images; p. 13 Andrew Aitchison/Corbis News/Getty Images; p. 14 Rob Marmion/Shutterstock.com; pp. 15, 17 CREATISTA/Shutterstock.com; p. 16 Varina C/Shutterstock.com; p. 18 Dima Sobko/Shutterstock.com; p. 19 Anutr Yossundara/Shutterstock.com; p. 21 Andrey_Popov/Shutterstock.com; p. 22 Monsterstock/Shutterstock.com.

Library of Congress Cataloging-in-Publication Data

Names: Felice, Frank (Children's writer), author.
Title: What happens when my parent is in jail? / Frank Felice.
Description: New York : PowerKids Press, [2019] | Series: Help me understand | Includes index.
Identifiers: LCCN 2017050220| ISBN 9781508167068 (library bound) | ISBN 9781508167082 (pbk.) | ISBN 9781508167099 (6 pack)
Subjects: LCSH: Children of prisoners–Juvenile literature. | Children of criminals–Juvenile literature. | Prisoners' families–Juvenile literature.
Classification: LCC HV8885 .F45 2019 | DDC 362.82/95-dc23
LC record available at https://lccn.loc.gov/2017050220

Manufactured in the United States of America

CPSIA Compliance Information: Batch #CS18PK: For Further Information contact Rosen Publishing, New York, New York at 1-800-237-9932

Contents

A Parent in Jail

People who break a law may have to go to jail. Jail is a **punishment** for doing something wrong. People can be in jail for a few days, a few months, or many years.

If you have a parent in jail, you're not alone. Thousands of children just like you have a parent in jail. Those kids have many of the same fears, worries, and feelings as you. It's important for you to remember that it was your parent who broke a law, not you.

You may not see your parent very often when they first go to jail. After a while, you'll be able to visit them.

5

Bad Choices

Laws are rules that help keep peace and order in **society**. Laws are created to keep people safe from harm and to make sure people are treated fairly. When a person breaks a law, he or she has done something that could be harmful or unfair to someone else.

Someone who breaks a law may have to go to jail as punishment. Breaking a law doesn't mean someone is a bad person. But it does mean they've made some bad choices.

People caught breaking a law often go to court. A judge listens to the case. The judge can send someone to jail if they're found **guilty**.

7

Time-Out!

Has your mom or dad ever put you in a time-out? This is when a child has broken a rule and is punished by having to sit quietly alone for some time. This gives the person who broke the rule a chance to think about what they did and why they did it.

Time-out is a little like jail. Both are a consequence of breaking a rule or law. People who go to jail have time to think about what they did and why it was wrong.

A consequence is something that happens because of something else. Time-out is a consequence of breaking a rule. Jail is a consequence of breaking a law.

Learning in Jail

Someone who's in jail is called a prisoner. Being in jail gives a prisoner a chance to think about why he broke the law. He can decide to change the way he acts so that he never breaks the law again.

Some jails have classes where prisoners can learn new job skills. Other classes help prisoners give up things that hurt them, such as drugs and alcohol. Prisoners can also learn how to be better parents.

The prisoners in this California jail are taking classes to become barbers when they're released from jail.

11

Time in Jail

The length of a prisoner's **sentence** depends on the law or laws they broke. However, other things can also affect how long a prisoner's sentence is. This includes if the person has been in jail before and the way that person acts while in jail.

No matter how long your parent is in jail, there will be changes in your life. Just remember that it's not your fault. Your parent still needs your love and support while they're in jail.

You will probably miss your parent while they're in jail. Going to visit them will help you keep in touch with them. ⟶

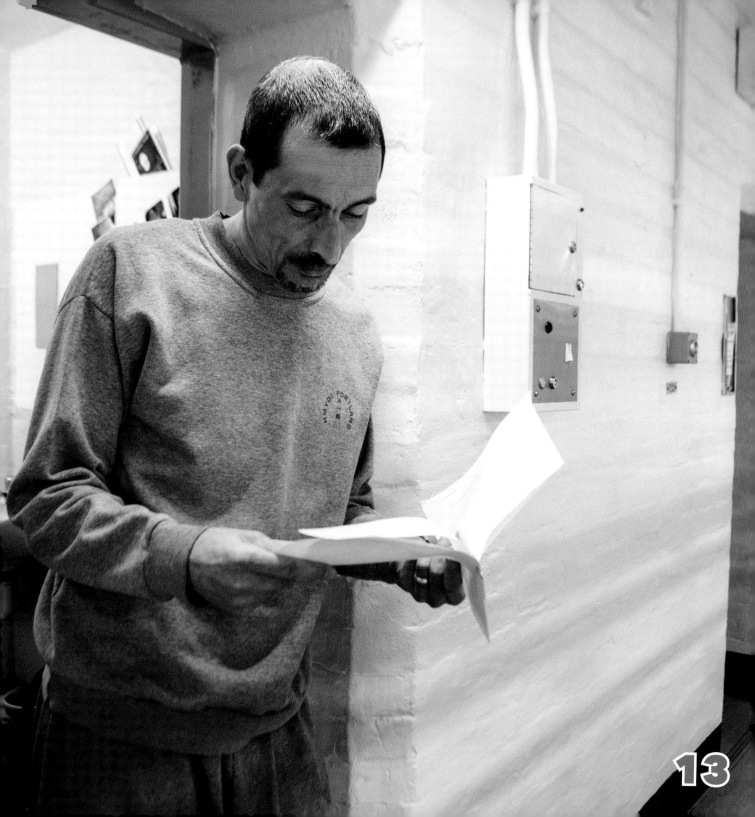

Family and Friends

Families face a lot of problems when a parent is in jail. You're sure to have changes in your life. Some of your friends, neighbors, and relatives may start to treat you differently. It's not fair, but they may try to make you feel bad about what your parent did.

Always remember that you and your family aren't to blame for the bad choices of one parent. Good friends and loving family members can help you deal with having a parent in jail.

True friends will be there for you while your parent is in jail.

Changes

With one parent in jail, there will be many changes in your family. Your family may have less money to pay bills with. It will be important for you to help out more often at home.

If your family doesn't have enough money, you may have to move. You may have to live with relatives, or you may have to live with a foster family. This can be a scary time. Just remember that people love and care about you. You'll be taken care of.

A foster family is a family that **volunteers** to take care of children who are in need. This can happen when a parent dies or when a parent is in jail.

17

Stay in Touch

You're sure to miss your parent when they're in jail, and they'll miss you too. The good news is that you can usually visit your parent in jail. Your other parent or another relative can help you find out how to visit your parent.

Even if you can't visit your parent, you can keep in touch with them. Your mom or dad will be very happy to receive letters from you. You may be able to call them, too.

It may be difficult to reach your parent on the phone. It may be easier for you to write them a letter.

19

Talk About Your Feelings

If you have a parent in jail, you're sure to have a lot of bad feelings about them. Someone you love did something wrong. You may feel angry, hurt, sad, ashamed, or **embarrassed**. You may miss your parent, and you may even feel guilty about what your parent did.

All of these feelings are normal. But remember that you did nothing wrong. Talking to your other parent can help you understand your feelings and how to deal with them.

You can talk to other relatives about your feelings. You can also talk to a teacher, coach, counselor, rabbi, or priest. ⟶

Homecoming

When your parent's sentence is over, they will be released from jail. Things will be different once they come home. You may need time to get to know your parent again. It may take some time for your parents and your family to feel comfortable with each other again.

It's important for you and your parent to talk openly with each other. Your parent made bad choices, but they've served their time in jail. Your parent needs your love. And they can help you avoid the same bad choices.

Glossary

embarrassed: To feel confused or foolish in front of other people.

guilty: Having done something wrong.

punishment: Something someone must do or a price they must pay for having done something wrong.

sentence: The length of time a prisoner is ordered to stay in jail.

society: A community, nation, or broad grouping of people having common traditions, activities, and interests.

volunteer: To do something to help because you want to do it.

Index

Websites

Due to the changing nature of Internet links, PowerKids Press has developed an online list of websites related to the subject of this book. This site is updated regularly. Please use this link to access the list: www.powerkidslinks.com/help/jail